Materials

KINGFISHER
LONDON & NEW YORK

First published as *Kingfisher Young Knowledge: Materials* in 2005
Additional material produced for Kingfisher by Discovery Books Ltd.

Distributed in the U.S. and Canada by Macmillan,
175 Fifth Ave., New York, NY 10010

Library of Congress Cataloging-in-Publication data has been applied for.

ISBN: 978-0-7534-6781-7

Kingfisher books are available for special promotions and premiums.
For details contact: Special Markets Department, Macmillan,
175 Fifth Ave., New York, NY 10010.

For more information, please visit www.kingfisherbooks.com

Printed in China
1 3 5 7 9 8 6 4 2
1TR/1211/UTD/WKT/140MA

Note to readers: the website addresses listed in this book are correct at the time of going to print. However, due to the ever-changing nature of the Internet, website addresses and content can change. Websites can contain links that are unsuitable for children. The publisher cannot be held responsible for changes in website addresses or content or for information obtained through a third party. We strongly advise that Internet searches should be supervised by an adult.

Acknowledgments
The publisher would like to thank the following for permission to reproduce their material. Every care has been taken to trace copyright holders. However, if there have been unintentional omissions or failure to trace copyright holders, we apologize and will, if informed, endeavor to make corrections in any future edition.
b = bottom, c = center, l = left, t = top, r = right

Cover: all images courtesy of Shutterstock.com ; 1 Getty Imagebank; 2–3 Alamy/Creatas; 4–5 Alamy/Greg Wright; 6–7 Getty Taxi; 8bl Corbis; 9cl Getty Photodisc; 9tr Getty Imagebank; 9br Getty Imagebank; 10l Getty Rubberball; 10–11 Getty Stone; 11tr Getty Brand X; 12bl Science Photo Library/Colin Cuthbert; 12r Alamy/Denis Hallinan; 13t Getty Stone; 13b Alamy/Sally Greenhill; 14–15 Corbis/Ron Watts; 14b Corbis/Lester Lefkowitz; 15b Getty Imagebank; 16c Corbis/Gary Braasch; 16b Getty Imagebank; 17 Corbis/Thomas Hartwell; 18b Corbis/David Samuel Robbins; 19t Photonica; 19br Alamy/Panorama Stock; 20–21 Getty Imagebank; 20b Getty Lonely Planet; 21tl Getty Brand X; 21br Rex Features; 22b Corbis/James Marshall; 23t Getty Photodisc; 23b NASA; 24 Corbis/Joel W. Rogers; 25t Getty Imagebank; 25bl Getty Brand X; 26 Getty Stone; 27tl Alamy/Troy and Mary Parlee; 27br Rex Features; 28cr Getty Stone; 28bl Corbis/Owen Franken; 29tl Alamy; 29b Corbis/Charles O'Rear; 30c Corbis/David H. Seawell; 30–31b Corbis/Patrik Giardino; 31tr Corbis; 31br Alamy/D. Hurst; 32–33t Corbis/Richard Hamilton Smith; 32bl Getty Imagebank; 32br Corbis/Wolfgang Kaehler; 33l Getty Imagebank; 33br Corbis/Ariel Skelley; 34bl Science Photo Library/Paul Whitehill; 34c Science Photo Library/Eye of Science; 35tl Corbis; 35b Corbis/Jim Cummins; 36bl Science Photo Library/Geoff Tompkinson; 37tl Corbis; 38 Getty Imagebank; 38b Corbis; 39tl Alamy/Dex Image; 39 Corbis/Ariel Skelley; 40b Getty Imagebank; 40r Getty Imagebank; 41tl Alamy/James Frank; 41r Getty Imagebank; 48 Alamy/Tim Brightmore; 48t Shutterstock Images/Gary Andrews; 48b Shutterstock Images/Charles Taylor; 49t Shutterstock Images/Michal Baranski; 49r Shutterstock Images/Svetlana Lukienko; 52 Shutterstock Images/Michaela Stejskalova; 53t Shutterstock Images/Anton V Pavlov; 53b Shutterstock Images/Elnur; 56 Shutterstock Images/RTimages

Commissioned photography on pages 42–47 by Andy Crawford
Thank you to models Cameron Green, Joley Theodoulou, and Hayley Sapsford

Materials

Clive Gifford

KINGFISHER
NEW YORK

Contents

What are materials? 6

Liquids and solids 8

Floating and sinking 10

Stretchy and flexible 12

Rocky world 14

Building blocks 16

Clay and ceramics 18

Using glass 20

Mighty metals 22

Mixing metals 24

Wonderful wood 26

Working with wood 28

The purpose of paper 30

Natural fabrics 32

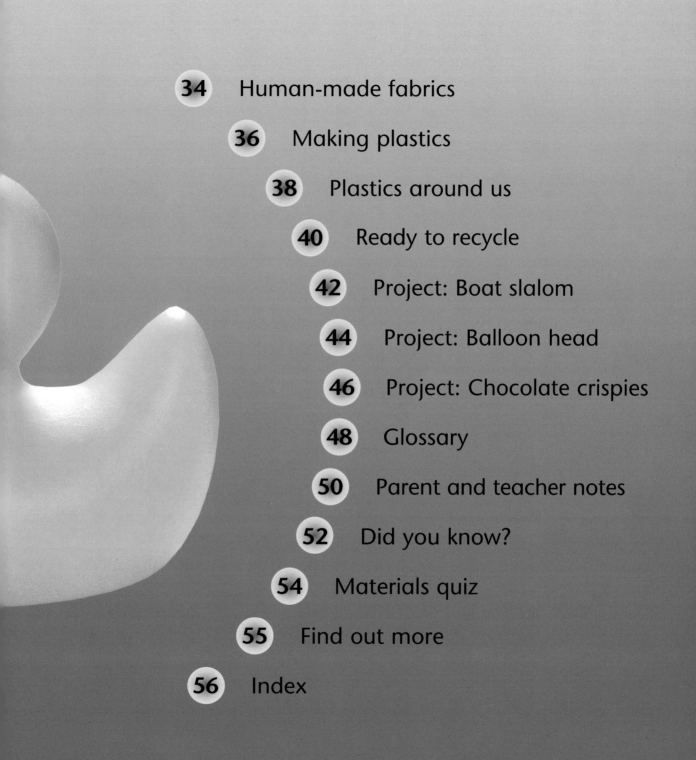

34 Human-made fabrics

36 Making plastics

38 Plastics around us

40 Ready to recycle

42 Project: Boat slalom

44 Project: Balloon head

46 Project: Chocolate crispies

48 Glossary

50 Parent and teacher notes

52 Did you know?

54 Materials quiz

55 Find out more

56 Index

What are materials?

Materials are all around us. They are the objects that make up the world in which we live. Some materials, such as rocks, are natural. Others—for example, plastic and glass—are made by people.

Using materials

People use materials all the time. This picture shows many different types. There are liquid paints, plastic paint bottles, and rollers, which are all human-made. There are also wooden shelves and a table, paper, and cotton clothing. These are made from natural materials.

Liquids and solids

Liquids are wet and can flow easily. Solid materials cannot flow and have a definite shape. Heat turns some solids into liquids.

Shaping shoes

Solid iron is heated to make it soft and easy to shape into a horseshoe.

Liquid gold

When gold is heated, it becomes a red, hot liquid that can be poured and shaped.

Hot chocolate ice cream

Ice cream can be dipped into warm, melted chocolate. Once cool, the chocolate gets hard and becomes a tasty treat.

Candlelight

A hot flame melts wax, which then runs down a candle. When the wax cools, it solidifies.

Melting Popsicle

In hot weather, you have to eat a Popsicle quickly before it melts. This is because the solid ice becomes watery when the sun warms it.

Floating and sinking

Some materials are very light and can float on water or even in the air. Other materials, such as rocks, are much heavier and normally sink.

Up, up, and away
Helium is a gas that is lighter than air. Balloons can be filled with helium to make them float in the air.

Sinking like a stone

Many materials, such as stones, are too heavy to float in water. This means that they sink to the bottom if they are thrown into a river or the ocean.

Floating fun

Both this raft and the children's life jackets are made of rubber. They float on water when filled with air. This means that they are great to play with in the ocean—and they keep you safe, too!

Stretchy and flexible

If you stretch or bend some materials, they return to their normal shape once you let go. Other materials stay in the shape you pull them.

Boing! Boing!

A spring is made of coiled wire. It jumps back to its usual shape after it has been squashed or pulled. That is why a pogo stick lets you bounce up and down.

High flier

Vaulting poles are very flexible and can bend a long way. They help athletes fly high up into the air.

Stretchy hair bands

Hair bands are often made of elastic. They stretch as they tie back long hair. Then they return to their normal shape and keep a perfect ponytail in place.

Rocky world

Rocks make up Earth's crust. They are ancient materials, and some are more than four billion years old. Rocks such as chalk are crumbly and soft, while others, such as granite, are hard and tough.

Hot rock

Burning hot lava comes from inside Earth. It is runny rock that turns hard as it cools.

Layer upon layer

Some rocks lie in layers called strata. Over millions of years, the layers can become bent, just like the sandstone in the picture.

Wear and tear

Cold, heat, water, and wind all wear away rocks little by little. Over time, amazing shapes, such as these arches, can form.

Building blocks

Rock is a very useful material that is strong, tough, and long lasting. It can be crushed up or used in big chunks to make buildings, roads, and statues, for example.

Mining for marble

Rock is mined in a quarry. Here, marble is being dug up. Marble is a hard rock that can be polished and used for floors and statues.

Big chunks

For centuries, rocks have been used to build walls. Giant blocks make up this old wall in Peru— they must have been very difficult to put in place.

Sparkling jewels

All rocks are made from minerals. Some minerals form beautiful and precious gemstones, such as these rubies and diamonds.

Living in the past

Rocks can be carved into sculptures that last a very long time. The Great Sphinx in Egypt was shaped from limestone rock around 4,500 years ago.

18 Clay and ceramics

Clay and ceramics are soft, earthy materials that are dug up out of the ground. They can be shaped easily. When they are heated, they dry out and become very hard.

Round and round

Clay can be shaped on a potter's wheel, such as the one below. Some clay objects dry out and harden in the sun. Others have to be fired in a hot oven called a kiln.

Perfect pools

Clay and ceramics are used to make tiles and bricks. Tiles form a smooth, waterproof surface that is perfect for lining swimming pools.

Pretty paints

Clay objects can be painted brightly. A liquid called a glaze is often brushed on. This makes the clay waterproof.

Using glass

Glass is mostly made from sand heated to a high temperature. While hot, glass can be shaped. For example, it can be pressed into windowpanes or blown into bottles.

Playing marbles

Some glass is very thin and breaks easily. Thick glass is strong and is great for making toy marbles.

Sealed in jars

Many foods, such as pickles, that contain liquids are kept in glass jars because they are waterproof and airtight. The food can be stored for years without going bad.

Glass of milk

Glass can be colored or clear (see-through). A lot of drinking glasses are clear so that you can keep an eye on what you are drinking.

With a huff and a puff

Glass objects can be made by glass blowing. A blob of runny glass is put on the end of a tube. Blowing into the tube inflates the glass like a balloon. When the glass cools, it sets hard.

Mighty metals

Metals are shiny materials found in rocks in the ground. Some metals are hard and tough. Others are softer and weak. Because they can be cut and bent, metals are used to make many different things.

Feeling the heat

Cooking pans are often made from metals such as copper. Heat can go straight through the metal to cook the food.

Glittering gold

Precious metals, such as gold, are valuable to people. They can be made into jewelry or shaped into bars called ingots that are worth a lot of money.

Traveling light

In 2004, two robots landed on the planet Mars. Parts of the robots were made from lightweight metals. This made the journey to Mars easier.

Mixing metals

Two or more metals—or a metal and a nonmetal—can be mixed together to form new materials called alloys. These alloys are useful because they can be light, strong, and very long lasting.

Space Needle

The Space Needle towers over the city of Seattle, Washington. It is made from steel, the world's most common alloy. Steel is used to make many things, from spoons to cars.

Not worth its weight in gold

In the past, coins were made
from precious metals such
as silver and gold. Now, they
are made from much cheaper
metals, often alloys.

As bold as brass

Brass is made from mixing
the metals zinc and copper.
It is tough and hard but
can still be shaped easily.
Many musical instruments
are made from brass.

Wonderful wood

Wood is a useful natural material. It comes from trees. Each type of tree is made of a different kind of wood— some are soft, and others are tough.

Collecting wood

Forest workers use cutting machines called chain saws to chop down trees. The trees are then cut up into logs.

To the sawmill

Logs are carried by trucks or floated down rivers. They are taken to a place called a sawmill. There, different sizes and thicknesses of wood are cut and prepared for use.

Soft landing

Leftover pieces of wood can be cut up into wooden chips. These are very soft, so they are often used in playgrounds.

Working with wood

Woodworking has been an important trade and a popular hobby for thousands of years. Today, wood is used to make many objects, including buildings, boats, and furniture.

Finely shaped

It is easy to cut and shape wood using tools. This person is working on a piece of wood with a metal tool called a chisel.

Family fun

Almost all wood floats on water. This means that it is very good for making rafts, boats, and ships.

Wooden pencils

Colored pencils are made from a long stick of color covered with a painted wooden case. Cedar wood is often used to make pencils because it is strong.

Bright beach huts

These wooden beach huts are brightly painted. The paint helps protect the wood from rain. If wood stays wet for a long time, it starts to rot and can fall apart.

The purpose of paper

Paper is a thin, lightweight material. It can be bent and folded easily. There are a lot of different uses for paper. Most often, it is used for writing or printing.

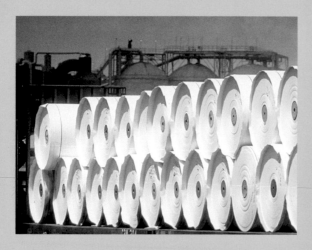

Making paper

Most paper is made in rolls in factories. It is usually produced from tiny pieces of wood, but it can also be made from rags or old paper.

Writing on paper

There are many types of writing paper. Notepaper is thin, and formal writing paper is thick. Greeting cards are stiff and stand up tall. All of these are smooth to write on.

Daily paper

Newsprint is a special type of paper used for newspapers. It is made from ground-up wood and is thin and cheap to produce.

Paper containers

Milk and juice cartons are made from paper. They are covered in plastic to make them waterproof. Many other papers, such as paper towels, soak up liquids.

Natural fabrics

Fabrics are made from long strands of material, called threads, that are woven together. Many threads come from plants and animals.

girls wearing kimonos

As smooth as silk

Silk is a beautiful fabric. It comes from thread spun by a silkworm while it is in its cocoon. It takes 3,000 cocoons to make a kimono.

Cotton buds

Cotton is a plant with big, fluffy buds called bolls. These are collected from fields and washed. They are then pulled into long threads and spun into fabric.

Warm wool

Wool comes from the coats of sheep and other animals, such as some goats and camels. It can be knitted into warm clothes and blankets.

Human-made fabrics

Some fabrics are not natural but are made from a natural raw material, such as coal. They are human-made and are called synthetic fabrics.

Velcro hooks and loops

Velcro is made from one strip of small hooks and another strip of tiny loops. The hooks catch in the loops when the strips are pressed together.

Flying high

Nylon is a light, strong fabric. It is used not only for clothing but also for ropes, fishnets, and even parachutes.

Synthetics in sports

Synthetic fabrics are often used to make sports clothing. This boy's shorts, tank top, and sneakers are all made from different lightweight fabrics.

Making plastics

Plastics are always human-made. People have learned to make them out of other substances, especially oil.

Plastic penguins

When heated, plastic can be shaped easily. It can be stretched and made into tubes or sheets, or it can be poured into molds to make objects, such as these toy penguins.

Creating bottles

To make a bottle, hot plastic is poured into a mold. A machine blows in air that presses the plastic to the sides of the mold. The cool plastic sets in a bottle shape.

Fabulous for food

Styrofoam is plastic foam. The foam is made by blowing bubbles of air into hot plastic. It keeps things warm and is lightweight— perfect for holding food.

Plastics around us

Plastic is used to make all sorts of objects, from furniture to paints and toys. Plastic does not rot quickly. This causes a problem with garbage. Reusing and recycling plastic helps cut down on waste (see page 40).

Toy blocks
Plastic blocks are long lasting, tough, and easy to clean. Many plastics are also cheap to make.

Beach life

Plastics can be very lightweight. Beach balls, balloons, and blow-up swimming pools are all made of plastic that can be filled up with air.

Singing in the rain

Plastic sheets can be cut and glued or sewn together to make brightly colored, waterproof clothes. This makes plastic an ideal material for raincoats, hats, and boots.

Ready to recycle

Many unwanted materials can be collected and turned into new materials. This is called recycling. Recycling helps cut down on waste.

the recycling symbol

Recycling at home

Many materials can be recycled—for example, glass, plastic, and paper. This family is sorting out its recycling trash. Each material goes into a different container.

Soda bottles to fleeces

A lot of fleece jackets are made from old soda bottles. The plastic bottles are shredded and turned into thread. About 25 bottles are needed for one fleece.

Swing time

Some items are reused rather than recycled. This old tire, for example, has been given a new job as a fun swing.

Boat slalom

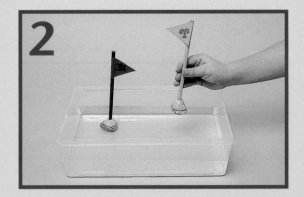

Blow a boat around a course
See how one material floats and another sinks with this fun and easy project.

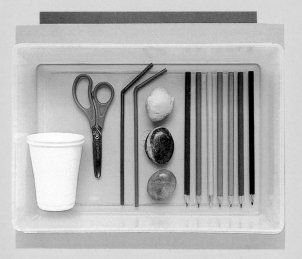

You will need:
- Waterproof modeling clay
- Two stones
- Two pencils
- Two triangles of cardboard, 1 x 1 x ¾ in. (3 x 3 x 2 cm), decorated with a picture
- Glue
- Wide, shallow container
- Water
- Scissors
- Plastic cup
- Drinking straw 4 in. (10 cm) long
- Square piece of colored paper, 2 x 2 in. (6 x 6 cm)

1 Press modeling clay onto a stone and push a pencil into the top of it. Glue the cardboard onto the end of the pencil as a flag. Now you have a slalom pole. Repeat.

2 Half fill the container with water and place the slalom poles in the middle of the bowl, with 4 inches (10 centimeters) between each. The poles should stick up out of the water.

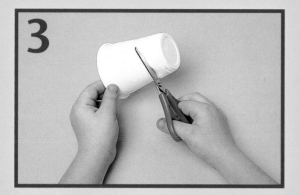

3

To make a boat, cut around a plastic cup, about 1 inch (2.5 centimeters) from its bottom. Stick modeling clay into the base.

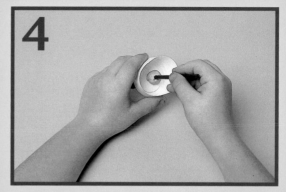

4

For the mast, push a plastic straw into the modeling clay so that it sticks straight up in the middle of the base of the cup.

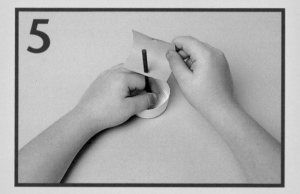

5

With scissors, make a small hole in the top and bottom of the colored paper. Push the paper onto the straw through the holes. You now have a sailboat that will float!

Put your boat at the start of the slalom course and blow it around the poles. Take turns with a friend to send your boat whizzing around the course.

Balloon head

Papier-mâché model
See how you can use many materials to create a sculpture of a head.

You will need:
- Newspaper
- Apron (optional)
- Balloon
- Balloon pump (optional)
- Plastic cup
- Strips of thin paper
- Colored paints
- Paintbrushes
- Bowl of ready-mixed four-and-water paste
- Glue
- Colored buttons
- Wool or silvery thread
- Marker

1 Cover a work surface with newspaper. Blow up the balloon. Place the knotted end of the balloon in a plastic cup.

2 Take a strip of paper, cover it in paste, and stick it onto the balloon. Continue doing this until the balloon is covered. Leave it to dry.

3

Repeat step 2 three more times so that your balloon is covered in four layers of paper strips. Let the head dry fully for a day.

4

Now paint your balloon head in a skin color—brown, pink, or white. Make sure the whole head is covered. Let the paint dry.

5

Decorate the papier-mâché balloon with wool or silvery threads for the hair and buttons for the eyes and nose. Color in a mouth using a marker. You could use other materials, such as paper hair, for more model heads.

Chocolate crispies

A tasty chocolate treat
See how chocolate can change from a solid into a liquid—and back into a solid again.

microwave not shown

You will need:
- Microwave
- Microwavable bowl
- 1 large bar of cooking chocolate (5 ounces or 150 grams)
- Large spoon
- 2.5 ounces (70 grams) Rice Krispies
- Small spoon
- Set of baking cups
- Plate
- Airtight container

1 Break up the bar of chocolate into single pieces and put them in the bowl. Microwave this for 90 seconds on full power.

2 Ask an adult to take the bowl out of the microwave and stir the chocolate. If it has not all melted, heat it for another 15 seconds.

Sprinkle the Rice Krispies on the melted chocolate. Stir the mixture until all of the rice is coated and the chocolate is used up.

Spoon a dollop of mixture into each baking cup and put them all on a plate to cool for an hour. Use up all of the mixture.

Once cooled and hardened, the chocolate crispies are ready to be stored in an airtight container . . .

. . . or eaten immediately!

Glossary

air—the mixture of gases that we breathe

airtight—closed to the air

arches—curved openings in rock

cedar—a large evergreen tree

chip—a small piece of a material after it has been cut or chopped

coal—a hard black rock found underground

cocoon—a covering around an insect made from silky thread

crust—the hard, rocky surface of Earth

elastic—a stretchy material

fired—baked at a very high temperature

flexible—bendable or stretchy

flow—to run like water

formal—proper or official

gas—a shapeless substance, such as air, that is not a solid or a liquid

ground-up—crushed into very fine pieces

human-made—made by people

inflates—fills with gas

iron—a strong, hard metal used to build or make things

lava—melted rock on Earth's surface

lightweight—not weighing much

limestone—a white rock that is used for building and making cement

mined—dug up out of the ground

mineral—a natural substance in Earth's rocks

mold—a hollow, shaped container

natural—found in nature, not human-made

oil—a thick, sticky liquid found underground

produced—made

raw material—a material used to make other materials

recycling—turning a material that is not needed into something that can be used again

rot—to go bad and fall apart

rubber—a tough, elastic material made from the milky fluid of a tropical plant

sandstone—a rock containing tiny grains of sand tightly packed together

shredded—cut up into very small pieces

silkworm—a type of caterpillar

solidifies—turns from liquid to solid

spun—twisted quickly

steel—a hard, strong alloy that is made by mixing the metal iron and the chemical carbon

substance—a material

trade—a job or business

valuable—worth a lot of money

The content of this book will be useful to help teach and reinforce various elements of the language arts and science curricula in the elementary grades. It also provides opportunities for crosscurricular lessons in math, mapping, design, and fine arts.

Extension activities

Written and oral language
Nylon and Dacron are familiar synthetic fabrics known for their strength. Other fibers such as Kevlar, Spectra, and Zylon are even stronger! Use reference materials to write a one- or two-page report about these stronger-than-steel fibers and how they are used. You might be surprised! Share your information in a short oral report.

Writing
If you could invent a completely new synthetic material, what would it look like? What would its properties be? What would you call it? Write one or two pages about your new material and how it would be used, both now and in the future.

Create a Venn diagram. To do this, draw a circle and label it "Made of Natural Materials." Draw another circle overlapping the first circle and label it "Made of Human-made Materials." Look around the room to find objects to list in each circle. Some objects, such as pencils, may be made of both types of materials. List these objects in the overlap between the circles.

Science
The topic of materials relates to the scientific themes of properties of matter, natural resources, manufacturing, technology and design, and the influence of engineering, technology, and science on society and the natural world.

Some specific links to the science curriculum include changes in the states of matter (pp. 8–9); floating and sinking (pp. 10–11); geology/Earth science (pp. 14–15, 16–17, 18–19, 22–23, 24–25); synthetic materials (pp. 34–35, 36–37, 38–39); and wood and wood products (pp. 26–27, 28–29, 30–31, 32–33).

Crosscurricular links

1) Writing, design, and art: Review the information about rocks, clay, glass, metals, wood, paper, plastics, and fabrics. If you were building a house, which materials would you use? Write one or two pages describing the design of your home and explaining your choice of materials. Include drawings showing the outside and the floor plan of your home.

2) Mapping: Take a walk down your street or a city block. Sketch a map showing the locations of at least six buildings. On a separate sheet of paper, list the materials that were used to construct each building.

3) Music/fine arts: Go to *www.bandfortoday.com/how-its-made* to find out about how different band instruments are made. Use materials from your home or classroom to create your own instrument that can be played.

4) Math/graphing: Go to your closet and take out the first 10–20 articles of clothing you see. Read the label of each to find out whether it is made of natural or synthetic fabrics. Display your data on a bar graph.

Using the projects

Children can do these projects at home. Here are some ideas for extending them:

Pages 42–43: Think of other materials that you could use for a boat in this project. Which materials would sink? Which would float? Make predictions and try them out.

Pages 44–45: Make a second balloon head, but this time use only natural materials to decorate it.

Pages 46–47: For a cheesy treat, make a nacho dip. Pour a can of evaporated milk into a microwavable bowl. Cut a half-pound (227-gram) block of Velveeta cheese into chunks and add it to the milk. Microwave for five minutes, or until the cheese is melted. Stir in a jar of mild salsa. Enjoy with corn chips!

Did you know?

- Diamonds are 90 times harder than any other natural substance found on Earth. Dentists' drills have a diamond coating.

- Gold is so soft and easily worked that you could roll 1 ounce (30 grams) of it into a hair-thin wire 50 miles (80 kilometers) long.

- In 2010, a rare 25-carat pink diamond became the most expensive jewel ever sold at auction. It was bought by a British man named Laurence Graff for about $46 million!

- An alloy is always harder than any of the materials from which it is made.

- Make sure you recycle all of the paper in your house. Every ton of paper recycled saves 18 trees.

- There are more than 4,000 types of minerals on Earth. Scientists are discovering new minerals all the time.

- Volcanoes eject melted rock called lava. The longest flow of lava ever measured was from Laki, a volcano in southern Iceland, in 1783. The lava stretched for almost 43 miles (70 kilometers)!

- Glass can form naturally. When lightning strikes sand, the heat sometimes fuses the sand into long, slender glass tubes called fulgurites. Another name for them is petrified lightning.

- Hardwoods come from deciduous trees (trees that lose their leaves), and softwoods come from evergreen trees (trees that don't lose their leaves).

- The hardest wood in the world comes from the Schinopsis tree of South America. Because of its hardness, the tree is nicknamed *quebracho*, which means "ax breaker" in Spanish. The wood is used to construct railroad ties.

- The coal we dig up from under the ground is formed from the remains of trees and plants that died up to 400 million years ago.

- One silkworm cocoon contains about 0.6 mi. (1km) of silk thread. Silk originally came from China, where its source was kept a secret for hundreds of years.

- Water is the only material in nature that can be a solid, a liquid, and a gas. When heated, solid ice melts into liquid water. Then it evaporates into the air as gas.

- An orange floats on water because the peel is full of trapped air pockets, making the orange light for its size. When you remove the peel, the orange weighs a lot for its size and it sinks in water.

- Wool is used in some unusual places. The covering on a tennis ball and the tip of a felt-tip pen are both made from wool.

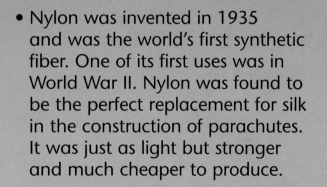

- Nylon was invented in 1935 and was the world's first synthetic fiber. One of its first uses was in World War II. Nylon was found to be the perfect replacement for silk in the construction of parachutes. It was just as light but stronger and much cheaper to produce.

- The most expensive oil used in perfumes is musk oil. It comes from the glands of male musk deer, which are found in the mountains of Asia. Amazingly, 2.2 pounds (1 kilogram) sells for about $44,000.

- On average, 323 plastic bags are taken into our homes every year, but one bag takes 500 years to rot when it is thrown away.

The answers to these questions can all be found by looking back through the book. See how many you get right. You can check your answers on page 56.

1) Which of these materials is not natural?
   A—Copper
   B—Cotton
   C—Plastic

2) Helium is . . .
   A—A liquid
   B—A gas
   C—A solid

3) What are layers of rock called?
   A—Strata
   B—Granite
   C—Lava

4) Which of these statements is not true?
   A—Some woods are soft, while others are very tough.
   B—Almost all wood floats on water.
   C—Wood is waterproof and does not rot.

5) Which material gets dry and hard when it is heated?
   A—Clay
   B—Limestone
   C—Marble

6) Plastic is made from which raw material?
   A—Wood
   B—Oil
   C—Coal

7) Glass can be shaped . . .
   A—While it is hot
   B—While it is cool
   C—On a potter's wheel

8) Which of these is not an alloy?
   A—A mixture of two metals
   B—A mixture of two nonmetals
   C—A metal and a nonmetal mixed together

9) Silk is a material created by which animal?
   A—Silkworm
   B—Silkslug
   C—Silkspider

10) Which of these is not a synthetic fabric?
   A—Wool
   B—Nylon
   C—Velcro

11) Which of these objects is not elastic?
   A—A spring
   B—A candle
   C—A hairband

12) Twenty-five soda bottles can be recycled into what?
   A—A newspaper
   B—A fleece jacket
   C—A tire

Books to read

Basher Science: Rocks and Minerals by Dan Green, Kingfisher, 2009

Changing Materials (Material World) by Robert Snedden, Heinemann, 2007

Changing Materials (Working With Materials) by Chris Oxlade, Crabtree, 2007

Gorgeous Gifts: Recycle Materials to Make Cool Stuff (Ecocrafts) by Rebecca Craig, Kingfisher, 2007

Minerals, Rocks, and Soil (Sci-Hi) by Barbara Davis, Raintree, 2009

Solids and Liquids (Essential Science) by Peter Riley, Franklin Watts, 2011

Places to visit

A. E. Seaman Mineral Museum, Houghton, Michigan
www.museum.mtu.edu
This museum houses more than 30,000 specimens of minerals from around the world. See the beauty of these natural materials and learn how they are mined and used by society. Special exhibits include native silver, datolite, Lake Superior agates, and greenstones.

Museum of Nature and Science, Dallas, Texas
www.natureandscience.org
This museum has a large section dedicated to children. It's a place where you will learn about the world we live in, whether natural or human-made. At the science discovery table, you can use your senses to explore minerals and other materials.

Paper Discovery Center, Appleton, Wisconsin
www.paperdiscoverycenter.org
Explore the world of paper at this science museum, including the history and technology of papermaking, recycling, and the vital role that paper plays in our lives. From historical photos of machines to samples of pulp and paper, there is a lot to touch, smell, and examine.

Websites

www.bbc.co.uk/schools/ks2bitesize/science/ materials/material_properties/play.shtml
Test your knowledge of materials in this entertaining activity.

http://familyfun.go.com/crafts/crafts-by- material/recyclable-projects
Use recyclable materials to make these fun crafts.

www.rocksforkids.com/RFK/howrocks.html
This website has a lot of information about rocks and minerals.

air 10, 11, 37, 53
alloys 24–25, 52
bending 12–13
building 16, 17, 28
cartons 31
ceramics 18–19
chocolate 9, 46, 47
clay 18–19
clothes 6, 32, 33, 35, 39, 40
coal 34, 52
coins 25
cold 9, 15, 21, 36, 47
cotton 6, 33
elastic 13
fabrics 32–33, 34–35
floating 10–11, 42–43
gases 10, 11, 21, 53
gemstones 17, 52
glass 6, 20–21, 40, 52
heat 8, 9, 15, 18, 20, 22, 36, 37

helium 10
jewelry 17, 23
lava 14, 52
liquids 6, 8–9, 20, 31, 46, 53
metals 22–23, 24, 25
mining 16
musical instruments 25
oil 36, 53
paper 6, 30–31, 40, 52
plastics 6, 31, 36–37, 38–39, 40, 41, 53
recycling 38, 40–41, 52, 53
rocks 6, 10, 14–15, 16–17, 22
rubber 10, 11
sand 20
silk 32, 53
sinking 10–11, 42, 53
solids 8–9, 46, 53
stretching 12–13
Styrofoam 37
water 10, 11, 15, 28, 42, 53
wood 6, 26–27, 28–29, 30, 52
wool 33, 53

Materials quiz answers

1) C
2) B
3) A
4) C
5) A
6) B
7) A
8) B
9) A
10) A
11) B
12) B